Chocolate
by Hershey

Chocolate by Hershey

A Story about Milton S. Hershey

by Betty Burford
illustrations by Loren Chantland

A Carolrhoda Creative Minds Book

Carolrhoda Books, Inc./Minneapolis

For Sarah and Andrew—B.B.
To my parents—L.C.

Special thanks to Pamela Cassidy, Hershey Community
Archives

Cover art based on photograph courtesy of Hershey Community
Archives. HERSHEY'S, HERSHEY'S KISSES, HERSHEY'S
MINIATURES, KRACKEL, and MR. GOODBAR are trademarks
of Hershey Foods Corporation and are used with permission.

This book is available in two editions:
Library binding by Carolrhoda Books, Inc.
Soft cover by First Avenue Editions
℅ The Lerner Group
241 First Avenue North
Minneapolis, Minnesota 55401

Library of Congress Cataloging-in-Publication Data

Burford, Betty.
    Chocolate by Hershey : a story about Milton S. Hershey / by Betty
Burford ; illustrations by Loren Chantland.
       p.   cm. — (A Carolrhoda creative minds book)
    Includes bibliographical references.
    ISBN 0-87614-830-5 (lib. bdg.)
    ISBN 0-87614-641-8 (pbk.)
    1. Hershey, Milton Snavely, 1857-1945—Juvenile literature.
2. Businessmen—United States—Biography—Juvenile literature.
3. Hershey Foods Corporation—History—Juvenile literature. 4. Chocolate
industry—United States—History—Juvenile literature. 5. Candy
industry—United States—History—Juvenile literature.
[1. Hershey, Milton Snavely, 1857-1945. 2. Confectioners. 3. Businessmen.]
I. Chantland, Loren, ill. II. Title. III. Series.
HD9200.U52H469 1994
338.7'664153'092—dc20
[B]   93-43638
                                                                    CIP
                                                                     AC

Manufactured in the United States of America
1 2 3 4 5 6 - I/MA - 99 98 97 96 95 94

Table of Contents

① Pennsylvania Farm Boy

Eastern Pennsylvania was a dangerous place that hot July of 1863. The Civil War had come as far as a little town called Gettysburg, and now there was a rumor that General Lee was going to march on Philadelphia. If the rumor was true, the Confederate army of the South could troop right through the Hershey farm. Five-year-old Milton Hershey lived with his parents and his younger sister, Serena, just forty miles from Gettysburg. The horrible, bloody war had torn the country apart, and now it had come to the Hersheys' doorstep.

Although they knew they couldn't stop the war from coming, many farmers in the area decided they could save their valuables by burying them. Milton wanted to save his valuables, too, so he scooted under his bed to get his precious matchbox full of pennies.

Milton carefully saved each penny he earned from running errands. And he planned to spend them—at the candy store. Milton loved all kinds of candy—sour balls, caramels, nougat, peppermints. . . . He was *not* going to risk losing his hard-earned cash, so he found a small shovel and began to dig behind one of the bushes lining the path to the back door. He slipped the box into the hole and covered it up with dirt. By the time he was finished, it was almost dark.

The next day, the Hersheys could hear the boom of cannon fire coming from the south. For three long days, the Hersheys and their neighbors waited in fear. They had no idea who was winning. Finally, word came that the Union troops of the North had won the battle, and the Confederates had retreated. The Hersheys could stop worrying, and life could return to normal.

On the morning after the battle, Milton dug furiously behind one bush after another. He couldn't remember exactly where he had buried the matchbox! The yard looked much different in daylight than it had at nightfall. Just then, his shovel struck something. He dug faster and unearthed his box—his pennies were safe. Milton couldn't wait to get to the candy store.

Milton Snavely Hershey was born on September 13, 1857, in an old stone farmhouse built by his great-grandfather near the little town of Derry Church, Pennsylvania. Milton's family belonged to a religious group called the Mennonites. His parents' ancestors had left their homes in Switzerland because their government required every able-bodied man to do military service. The Mennonites were peace-loving people and didn't believe in war. Many of them came to the rolling hills of Pennsylvania, where William Penn had promised religious freedom, and followed their sober way of life. They dressed in plain clothes, worked hard, and avoided most common forms of entertainment—they did not dance or play cards or go to the theater. They felt it was wrong to read for pleasure, and their only reading was the Bible.

Milton's mother, Fanny Hershey, taught young

Milton these Mennonite beliefs. She taught him the Golden Rule—do to others as you want them to do to you. She also taught him to work hard and to be careful with money.

Henry Hershey, Milton's father, was not a typical Mennonite farmer. He loved to read and was a great talker. He read about faraway places, unusual facts, and how things worked. He always had some new scheme in his head. Henry kept trying new ideas on the farm, such as planting fruit trees or raising trout. He had some good ideas, but he didn't have the money to see them through—there was never much money at the Hershey household.

Fanny's sister, Mattie Snavely, had no use for Henry. She didn't approve of Henry's ideas or that he didn't like to stay in one place for very long. Mattie never married, and she lived with her brothers, Abe and Ben, on the Snavely family farm near Lancaster, about thirty miles from Derry Church. Mattie dearly loved her nephew, Milton, and the two sisters, Mattie and Fanny, were close friends throughout their lives.

Milton loved his parents equally, but he realized that he could never be the serious, sober Mennonite that his mother was. He loved fun too much.

Milton knew that hard work came before having fun. He helped out on the farm every day, feeding the chickens, driving the cows to pasture, and doing other chores. But Saturday was the day of the week he liked best. On Saturday his father loaded the wagon with eggs, butter, and vegetables, and the whole family set out for the market at nearby Harrisburg. While Fanny waited on customers and took care of Serena, Henry chatted with anyone and everyone who stopped by. Then came the moment Milton had waited all week for— he was allowed to go to the candy store. Each week the hardest part was deciding which delicious treat to choose.

When Milton was seven, he started his education at the one-room schoolhouse in Derry Church. The students sat on long benches, and when the teacher's back was turned, the boys played a game called "scrouging." The boys in the middle pushed the boys next to them, each one pushing, till the boys at the ends of the bench fell on the floor.

The next year, when he was eight, Milton went to the Rockridge School. Milton had not done well at Derry Church, and he didn't do any better at the new school. He wasn't much of a student, and it didn't help that the Hersheys kept moving.

By the time Milton was nine, they had moved several times because his father could not stay in one place for long.

When Milton was eleven, tragedy struck the Hershey family. Milton's little sister Serena died. From that time on, Fanny put all her hopes in Milton. She wanted him to make a success of his life. Perhaps she had extra hope for Milton because Henry could never quite make his ideas work.

② Learning a Trade

Henry Hershey had dreams for Milton, just as Fanny did. He was determined that Milton should get a good education so his son could be more than a farmer or a common worker. But Milton's mother and his aunt Mattie realized that Milton was not going to do well in school, especially if they kept moving. By the time he was thirteen, Milton had been to six different schools. Both Fanny and Mattie agreed that he should learn a trade.

In those days, young workers learned a trade from someone who knew it, and they usually lived with their teacher. This was called an apprenticeship. Henry finally agreed that Milton could stop going to school, but in exchange, he set up an apprenticeship for Milton with a newspaper editor named Sam Ernst. Milton's father thought newspaper work was a noble profession for his son—it had to do with ideas and words.

Besides publishing the newspaper, Mr. Ernst ran a mill and did some farming. Milton helped with the cows and set type for the newspaper. Each letter of type was made of metal, and Milton set the letters into words on a long metal tray called a galley. The galley was put into the printing press, the press was inked, and paper was fed through to print the newspaper.

Sam Ernst was a hot-tempered man who would not put up with mistakes or clumsiness. Unfortunately, Milton was sometimes guilty of both. One day when Milton dropped a galley of type, Mr. Ernst got especially angry. He exploded and kept on yelling. Milton had a hot temper, too. He pulled off his straw hat, which landed right in the press. The press jammed, and that was the end of Milton's apprenticeship. He was fired!

Milton returned home worried about how his parents would react to his failure. His father grabbed his coat and left to talk Sam Ernst into taking Milton back. But Milton's mother and his aunt Mattie had other plans. Fanny thought Milton should learn to make something he could sell, and Mattie agreed. Although Sam Ernst agreed to give Milton a second chance, young Milton Hershey became an apprentice to a new trade.

This time the trade was confectionery, or candy making. Milton left home for Lancaster, Pennsylvania, to work with Joe Royer at his Ice Cream Parlor and Garden. He would spend four years learning how to make delicious things: candy, ice cream, and cakes.

From the very first day at Joe Royer's, Milton felt he had found what he wanted to do with his life. He loved making candy. There were no exact recipes, so he had to rely on his taste buds. Mr. Royer taught him to start with sugar, the basic ingredient in candy. Then he added water or milk, depending on the kind of candy he was making, and boiled it in a kettle. Milton learned to judge the exact moment when the copper kettle should be taken off the fire. Then Milton poured the hot syrupy mixture onto a marble slab, where he worked it with a large wooden paddle, pulling the candy back and forth as it cooled.

Milton learned what flavors appealed to most people, and he learned just how much peppermint or vanilla or almond to add to make a batch of candy taste just right. He found he had a gift for knowing exactly what to add to any candy mixture to make it better.

Milton occasionally made mistakes, of course.

But unlike Sam Ernst, Joe Royer was patient. One night Milton went with some friends to the Fulton Opera House, near Royer's. His eyes were glued to the stage, when all at once he smelled something burning. That something was peanuts—Milton had been roasting peanuts for fudge and had forgotten to turn off the machine! He rushed down to the candy shop and found peanut shells blowing around and an awful smell in the air. Mr. Royer forgave him this mistake and others, and came to regard Milton as a hard worker he could depend on.

In May 1876, after four years of hard work and learning, Milton Hershey thought it was time to go into the candy business for himself. He talked to his mother and his aunt about his prospects. Although Milton was only eighteen years old, Fanny and Mattie both agreed he should try to make it on his own.

Milton didn't consult his father this time. Henry was hardly ever around. Milton's mother and father no longer lived together—they were just too different from each other. Milton's father was still part of Milton's life, but he tended to come and go. As much as he loved his father, Milton realized that his mother and Aunt Mattie were the family he could count on.

Aunt Mattie presented Milton with $150 to start his own business. Fanny wanted him to stay in Lancaster, but Milton had grander ideas. The United States was celebrating its hundredth birthday, and the city of Philadelphia was hosting a world's fair in honor of the event. The fair would run from May till November and would celebrate the industries of all nations. Milton decided Philadelphia was the place for him.

③
Milton S. Hershey, Confectioner

Milton rented a small, brick shop on Spring Garden Street in Philadelphia, where he could live and make candy. He borrowed Uncle Abe's wagon and loaded it high with furniture and the candy-making equipment he had bought in Lancaster. His mother and Aunt Mattie moved to Philadelphia to help him, and in June of 1876 Milton put up his sign, "Milton S. Hershey, Confectioner."

Milton worked very hard. Often at midnight he was still boiling, cutting, and wrapping candies. Each candy sold for a penny, but this turned out to be a problem—as hard as he worked, Milton couldn't make candies fast enough to make a profit. But if he raised the price, they would be too expensive and no one would buy them.

Another problem with Milton's new business was that he tried to sell too many products. One of the many kinds of candy he made was called "French Secrets." The wrapper of each candy had a verse on it, such as "Roses are red, violets are blue, sugar is sweet, and so are you." Besides the different kinds of candy, Milton was also making ice cream and selling nuts. He was so excited about his new business, perhaps he tried to please everyone by making a wide variety of treats. But he wasted time and energy trying to do it all.

Milton decided he needed some extra help, so in 1880 he hired a man named William Lebkicher, known as Lebbie, who had been working as a carpenter in Lancaster. He was a tall, lean man of few words and a very hard worker. "I could outtalk Lebbie," Milton said later, "but I could never outwork him."

Lebbie used a horse and wagon to make deliveries to stores that sold Milton's candies. One day, not long after he left on his rounds, Lebbie reappeared at the shop on Spring Garden Street with his clothes torn and his arm bleeding.

The horse had been frightened and had bolted, Lebbie explained to Milton, and the wagon overturned, dumping all the candy into the street. Every kid on the block came running, and quick as a wink, the candies disappeared.

But even with Lebbie's help, Milton was still overworked and worried about money. Aunt Mattie wrote constantly to Uncle Abe asking for help. "Please send four hundred dollars," she would write. "We need it to pay for sugar."

Soon Milton fell ill. While he was too sick to work, his mother, Aunt Mattie, and Lebbie kept the business going. The bills kept coming in, though, and there was never enough money. Sugar dealers would not give credit—they demanded payment on delivery. And the stores that sold Milton's candy were slow to pay what they owed him. Finally, discouragement won out, and Milton decided to give up on Philadelphia. Six years after he had begun business in Philadelphia, he borrowed Uncle Abe's wagon again and returned to Lancaster. Milton was twenty-five years old, broke, and out of business. He had no idea what to do next.

Milton soon heard from his father, who had gone to Colorado to seek his fortune. Henry wrote telling of all the marvelous opportunities in the West and urging his son to join him as soon as possible. Milton took the train to Denver. He soon discovered that he loved the majestic Rocky Mountains and great stands of pine trees. Now he just needed to find a job.

Milton found work with a candy maker who specialized in caramels. Although making candy is much the same everywhere, Milton knew right away that these were not ordinary caramels. In fact, these were among the most delicious caramels Milton had ever tasted. In addition to sugar and vanilla, they contained a secret ingredient—fresh milk. Milton's new boss explained that milk made them extra chewy and kept them fresh much longer.

Milton enjoyed his work making caramels, and he had learned about an important new ingredient. But in a way, he felt as if he were right back in Lancaster working for Joe Royer. Milton was working for someone else, and he still wanted to be his own boss.

On the move again, Henry Hershey left Denver to work in Chicago as a carpenter, and Milton followed him there in 1883. Milton wanted to start his own business again, so he talked his father into teaming up with him. But after only three short months, the business ground to a halt. Henry had some money problems and had to withdraw from candy making.

Milton was frustrated, but he wasn't giving up that easily. He decided to try again, this time in the south, so he took the train to New Orleans. Unfortunately, he reached a dead end before he even started—there was no candy-making equipment to be had in New Orleans. He would have to send to New York for it and pay the freight for its delivery. Why not just go there himself? Once again, Milton boarded a train, this time for New York City.

Milton soon got a job at Huyler's, a well-known candy maker. Every day he made whatever candy his boss wanted him to make. But every evening after work, he borrowed his landlady's kitchen and became his own boss. Most nights he boiled up a big batch of taffy. Taffy needs to be pulled. So when it had cooled, Milton wrapped the rope of candy around a big hook in the wall and pulled it until it was light in color and just the right texture. Then he cut the taffy into pieces, wrapped it, and put it in a basket. With the basket on his arm, he stood under a bright street lamp to sell his candy. In a very short time, Milton had enough money to buy a big steam kettle. He was ready to try business for himself again.

Milton rented a new shop, and, once again, his mother and Aunt Mattie came to help him. Even his father returned from the West to join in the business. Milton worked harder and harder. But just as before, he had trouble making a profit. He couldn't borrow any more money from Aunt Mattie, since she had lent him all she had, and his uncles in Pennsylvania refused to part with another dime.

One day a man who sold cough drop machinery came into Milton's shop. The man offered to let Milton have the machinery if he promised to pay him ten thousand dollars at a later date. Maybe a new product would help turn Milton's business around. Milton decided to take a risk. He promised to pay the man back and feverishly set to work making cough drops. Time went by, and Milton worried as the day to repay the money came closer. Finally, the due date came, but Milton had not made enough money. His risk didn't pay off. The salesman summoned a sheriff, and the cough drop machinery was taken away.

Milton was in despair. He sadly scraped together enough money to send his mother and aunt home.

Then he packed up the equipment he had left and sent it to Lancaster, the cost of shipping to be paid on arrival. Milton had just enough money left for his own railroad ticket home.

When the train finally pulled into the Lancaster station, Milton's troubles were far from over. His uncles' farm was seven miles south of town—and Milton was on foot. The long hike gave him plenty of time to rehearse what he would say to Uncle Abe and Uncle Ben when he got there. He was *sure* he could make a go of things if he could just have one more chance. Candy making was the one thing in the world he wanted to do, and he knew he was good at it. He decided that next time he would make just one kind of candy—caramels. And he would use fresh milk, as he'd learned to do in Denver. But when he got to the farm, his uncles wouldn't listen. To make matters worse, they didn't even offer him a bed for the night. Feeling miserable, Milton began the long haul back to Lancaster.

It was quite late by the time Milton plodded into town, and he was tired, cold, and above all, discouraged. Then he remembered that William Lebkicher lived on Queen Street. Maybe good old Lebbie was still up. It was worth a try.

Not only was Lebbie still awake, but he took Milton in. Milton was grateful for the warm welcome. But he was even more grateful when Lebbie offered to pay the freight on Milton's equipment. Then Lebbie suggested that after a good night's sleep they look for a place to start again in the candy business.

④

The Best Caramels in the World

Lebbie Lebkicher was as good as his word—he gave Milton the money he needed, and together they looked for a place to make candy right at home in Lancaster. They found it in a factory building that belonged to a man named Jake Gable, and Milton was in business again. With the help of his mother, Aunt Mattie, and Lebbie, Milton began making caramels. They were of the highest quality, and, of course, milk was the secret ingredient.

Milton started out selling his candy from a pushcart, but he wondered how he could expand his business. Surely people would want his tasty new caramels. About this time, a candy importer from a company in England came to Lancaster and found his way to Milton's shop. The Englishman had tried Milton's caramels and thought they were the best he had ever tasted. He wanted more of these wonderful caramels and asked Milton if he could send large batches to England. Milton was thrilled! This was the marvelous break he needed. Now he would have large orders he could depend on—he wouldn't have to rely on sales from his pushcart.

But in order to fill the English company's large orders, Milton would have to expand. He needed bigger kettles, more space, more employees. In other words, he needed money.

Milton had tried almost all of the banks in Lancaster in an effort to get a loan, but without success. Just one bank was left. Milton pleaded with Mr. Brenneman, the cashier at the Lancaster National Bank. He told him about his earlier business ventures, explaining that this was his chance to make it big. Perhaps Brenneman was impressed by Milton's refusal to quit, or perhaps it was Milton's enthusiasm. Whatever it was, Mr. Brenneman was persuaded, and the bank lent Milton seven hundred dollars for ninety days. Loyal Aunt Mattie promised to give the bank her little house if Milton couldn't pay.

Now the factory began to hum in earnest. Milton

hired more workers, the kettles bubbled, and the finished candies were quickly wrapped and packed, ready to ship to England. The import company sent even bigger orders, but Milton worried about paying off the loan. He had to wait for the caramels to get to England before his payment would come back. Soon the ninety days were up, and the money from England still had not come. Milton couldn't pay.

Empty-handed, Milton trudged off to talk to Brenneman at the bank. But Milton was not going to let his big chance slip away. He told Mr. Brenneman that not only was he unable to repay the seven hundred dollars, but he needed a thousand more to keep up with the orders from England. Milton begged Brenneman to come to the factory and see his candy-making operation. Once again, Milton managed to persuade him. Mr. Brenneman gave his approval for the additional thousand-dollar loan as well as for more time for the first loan.

Milton quickly bought more equipment and made even larger shipments to England. Milton was hard at work boiling caramels about ten days before the loans came due, when a letter with foreign stamps on it arrived. Milton tore open the envelope to find a check for $2,500! He grabbed his coat and hat and raced to the bank. Halfway there, he realized he was still wearing his candy-spattered apron. He tucked it under his jacket and triumphantly presented his deposit to the teller at the bank.

From that day on, Milton Hershey's Lancaster Caramel Company was sure of success. Before long, caramel making took over the entire factory building, and Milton needed money to expand. Mr. Brenneman told Milton that only a really big bank could give him the kind of loan he needed, so he took Milton to New York City. Milton wanted to ask for $100,000, but to his amazement, the New York banker offered him $250,000. Milton was delighted.

After only four years of business in Lancaster, Milton's caramels seemed to be a hit with everyone. He called them CRYSTAL A, and stamped this name on every box. Though Milton stuck to his decision to manufacture only caramels, he experimented with various shapes and sizes and flavors. For example, he made bean-shaped MC-GINTIES, which sold ten for a penny, and LOTUSES, his fanciest caramels made not just with milk, but cream as well. Milton invented all of these candies himself.

Milton Hershey always seemed to be in a hurry. Running a candy factory was no small job. CRYSTAL A Caramels were eaten in places all over the world—Japan, China, Australia, Europe. When success finally came, it came in a big way. In 1894 the Lancaster Caramel Company did over a million dollars' worth of business. A history of Lancaster County published that year said, "Milton S. Hershey has made a complete success of his life thus far, and is the president of the largest concern of this kind in the world."

Milton was grateful to all the people who had helped his company succeed—especially his employees. Milton seemed to have a knack for finding hardworking, dedicated employees. He expected a lot out of them, and he set an example for them with his own hard work.

At last Milton could put poverty and worries about money behind him. He bought a large yellow house with white trim for himself and his mother and decorated it with elegant furniture. He planted beautiful gardens and even installed a fountain with a spray of water that balanced a ball on top. The neighborhood children thought it was wonderful.

Milton's mother worried that he was spending too much money and would come to ruin. She warned him, "Be careful, Milton. You know how easy it is to get into debt." But Milton relished his newfound success and the fine things he could now buy. Milton was thirty-seven years old. He decided it was time to visit England to see how his caramels were being sold.

⑤

Love and Chocolate

Milton discovered that the English candy company was cutting the bulk caramels imported from Lancaster into bite-sized pieces. They then dipped the caramels in chocolate, wrapped them, and put their own name on them. Milton learned that not only caramels but also all kinds of "centers"—nuts, cordial cherries, nougat, and toffee—were being dipped in chocolate. They were a treat for wealthy people.

One day while Milton was in England, he was invited to a garden party. There was a lavish spread of cakes and little sandwiches, and as a special treat, dipped chocolate confections. The children at the party took their chocolates and ran off with them. Milton was curious. He followed the youngsters to where they were hiding behind a hedge. Milton wondered what on earth was going on. As he watched, the children licked the chocolate coating off the candies and spit out the centers! They didn't care what was in the center, they liked the chocolate.

Milton had always wanted to make candy for children. Maybe he should think about making chocolate—children obviously loved it. But he would need to make sure children could afford it. He never forgot how he saved his own precious pennies for candy. Milton put this thought away for the future.

Back in the United States, it was world's fair time once again, and Milton eagerly headed to Chicago for the festivities. Most fair-goers headed straight for George Ferris's huge new wheel with seats that took passengers high into the air. But Milton's nose led him to an exhibit of chocolate-making machinery from Germany. Milton returned to the exhibit again and again—the machinery was spellbinding.

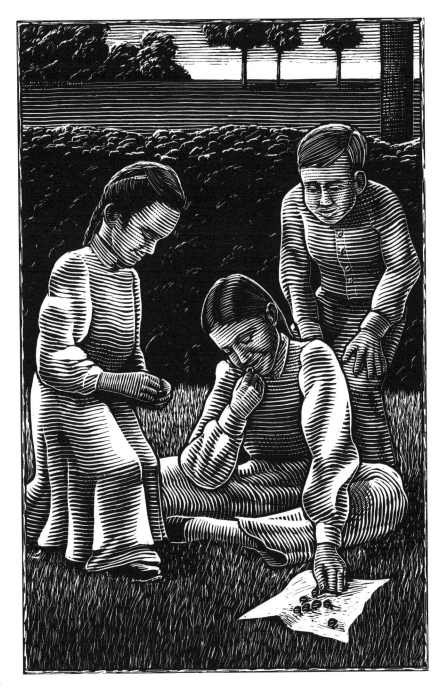

39

Chocolate making started with cocoa beans, which came from the tropical cacao tree. A roaster cooked the beans, a hammering table knocked their shells off, and a grinding machine mashed the beans into a rich, dark liquid called chocolate liquor. This liquor, which contains no alcohol, is the base for all chocolate products. To make cocoa powder for baking, a large press squeezed the liquor until a fat called cocoa butter was pressed out. This extra cocoa butter could then be added back to chocolate liquor along with sugar to make rich and tasty chocolate candy.

Milton was so excited by chocolate making that he bought the display machinery and shipped it back to Lancaster when the fair ended. He remembered the children in England who loved chocolate. He wanted to make chocolate for children—and he was sure it would sell.

So in a corner of the Lancaster Caramel Company, Milton began experimenting with chocolate. He hired two experienced chocolate makers to teach him how to run the machinery. Now he could make his own chocolate to flavor and coat his caramels. But he also began making some purely chocolate products.

Milton had to decide which cocoa beans to use,

how much sugar and flavoring to add, how long to mix the chocolate. Each one of these important decisions made a difference in the flavor and texture of the chocolate. Then Milton molded the finished chocolate into candies of all different shapes and sizes. Before long, his delicious new treats were ready to sell—and eat. He proudly presented HERSHEY'S Cocoa, HERSHEY'S Baking Chocolate, and his fancy chocolate candies.

Only one cloud shadowed his new project. In April of 1894, Aunt Mattie fell ill. At first it didn't seem serious, but she grew worse. After only a few days, she died. Her death was a great blow to Milton. He owed much of his success to his faithful aunt Mattie. He missed her very much.

Still, Milton could not let his unhappiness interfere with the large business he had to run. He traveled all over, visiting small candy stores and trying to get them to sell his caramels and his brand-new chocolate products. He especially enjoyed visiting a store in Jamestown, New York, and he returned to it more often than he needed to. A saleswoman there, Miss Catherine Sweeney, known as "Kitty," was the cause of these frequent visits. Milton thought she was beautiful. He especially liked her auburn hair and flashing smile.

Milton wrote to her often, and he sent her a special box of chocolates he had made and wrapped himself for her birthday. He began to think of her as "my Kitty." Even though Milton was quite a bit older than Kitty, he got his courage up, and the next time he was in Jamestown, he asked her to marry him. To his delight, Kitty said yes, and they were married in May of 1898 in New York City.

Milton and Kitty returned to Lancaster, and Milton was happier than he thought was possible. His father was back in Pennsylvania and seemed settled at last. With his family around him and Kitty at his side, Milton was ready to do even greater things. He had big plans, and they all involved chocolate.

⑥

The Chocolate Factory in the Cornfield

On August 10, 1900, Lancaster's afternoon newspaper carried a huge headline:

CARAMEL FACTORY SOLD
MILTON S. HERSHEY RECEIVES
A MILLION DOLLARS FOR IT!

The headline was true. The Lancaster Caramel Company was so successful that other caramel makers wanted Milton to go into business with them. When he refused, they offered to buy him out for one million dollars, and he took their offer.

But Milton wasn't giving up on candy making—far from it. He was busy working on a brand-new scheme. Since making just one product had worked so well with caramels, he decided it was time to try it again. Milton Hershey was ready to give chocolate his undivided attention.

When Milton sold the caramel factory, he kept the chocolate-making machinery and the rights to make chocolate. His chocolate company was already doing well at this point. In fact, after much experimenting, he had even discovered how to make milk chocolate—creamy tasty chocolate with milk that the Swiss had made with a secret recipe. So in 1900, Milton introduced his brand-new HERSHEY'S Milk Chocolate Bar.

Milton bought his first automobile—indeed, the first auto in Lancaster—and painted "Hershey's Cocoa" on the side to advertise his chocolate. His salesmen drove the electric car around Lancaster and the surrounding towns at its fastest speed of nine miles per hour. This caused quite a stir and brought in lots of orders. Milton felt sure that people in the rest of the country—and the world—would want his chocolate products.

If Milton was going to make chocolate for everyone, he would have to mass-produce it—in other words, he would have to make lots and lots of chocolate. He would need a huge new factory. When Milton made up his mind, he acted on it right away, and he had made up his mind to build a giant new chocolate factory.

The first step was deciding where to put it. Each of Milton's top employees had a different idea about where to build, but Milton decided that right at home in Derry Church was the perfect place.

Most people thought Milton was crazy, but most people did not have his vision. In the middle of what was then a cornfield, he saw a factory. Beyond the factory would be plenty of pastureland for the cows that would provide milk for the chocolate. The railroad already ran through Derry Church, so Milton could bring in cocoa beans and sugar and send out chocolate. Surrounding the factory, he would build an entire town for his employees to live in. (Milton would need to employ about six hundred workers.) He would run trolley lines to Lancaster and other nearby towns so workers could live elsewhere if they wanted to.

Milton wanted to get to work right away, and in 1903 the ground was broken for the six-acre factory. Meanwhile, the town was laid out. The center of town was the intersection of Chocolate and Cocoa Avenues. Around the center, streets named for the places cocoa beans came from—Trinidad, Java, Caracas—were laid out for houses. Milton told his architect not to make the houses all alike and to give each one a garden. He made sure the houses were reasonably priced so the workers could own their own homes. Milton wanted his workers to be happy. He knew that in order to have a good workforce, he needed to treat his employees generously.

The town needed more than just houses. Schools, churches, a bank, and a store went up. Milton wanted to provide recreation and entertainment for the townspeople as well. He built an amusement park, golf courses, a zoo, a dancing pavilion, and, a bit later, an outdoor theater.

Milton's family took part in the bustle and activity as the factory and town took shape. Milton's mother and Kitty visited often, and no one was prouder of Milton than his father. "Milton is thinking big," Henry told Lebbie. "That's the way to do things." Unfortunately, Henry Hershey did not live to see the factory completed. He died in February of 1904. But he died knowing that his son was well on his way to making his biggest dream of all a success.

Soon the new factory was in full production. Before long Milton's chocolate was being sold all over the United States, and the business was an even bigger success than anyone could have dreamed—except, of course, Milton Hershey. No other chocolate company anywhere could compete with his.

Milton was an attentive boss and a fair one. He wanted to keep an eye on the factory night and day. So on a hill across a small creek from the factory, Milton and Kitty built a new house they called High Point. Kitty laid out extensive gardens and furnished the mansion with treasures collected on their travels. The Hersheys enjoyed entertaining in their new home. They loved having their friends around them.

Milton Hershey wanted to share his town with more people—he was sure it could be a tourist attraction. He persuaded the Philadelphia and Reading Railroad to build a passenger station, and thousands of visitors soon were able to visit the growing town by rail. Every weekend the trolley line and the railroad featured special excursion fares to the chocolate town. In 1906 the town officially changed its name from Derry Church to Hershey in honor of Milton, and the name became a symbol not only for delicious candy but also for fun. Much later, even the streetlights were shaped like silver-wrapped HERSHEY'S KISSES, a chocolate treat first produced in 1907. Milton and Kitty loved the way the town was turning out. They especially enjoyed what the factory workers jokingly called "the stink"—the fragrant aroma of chocolate.

The Hershey Chocolate Company continued to grow rapidly and make bigger and bigger profits, and in just a few years the Hersheys were richer than ever. Even though Milton expanded the plant and made additions to the town, he couldn't possibly spend all the money he had. Milton Hershey had always felt that one ought to share good fortune. He had certainly shown that in his generosity to the town of Hershey, but with so much money he wanted to do more.

The Hersheys had always been sad that they were unable to have children. When Kitty suggested that they start a home for orphan boys, Milton welcomed the idea and immediately began planning. Milton wanted the boys to go to school as well as learn a trade. That way they could support themselves when they finished school.

The first two boys to attend the Hershey Industrial School were brothers, four and six years old.

Their father had died and their mother could not afford to care for them. They lived and attended classes at the old Hershey Homestead, the family farm. The school grew rapidly, but the central idea stayed the same. Milton felt that a homelike atmosphere was very important, and he hired kind houseparents to live with the boys. The school provided everything the boys needed.

As a part of their education, Milton wanted to be sure the boys learned to work hard, as he had when he was a boy. They learned how to farm and helped with chores around the Homestead. But it wasn't all work. Swimming in the summer and ice-skating in the winter were favorite sports, and the students loved the amusement park.

Milton loved to visit the students. Kitty, though, wasn't able to visit often, as she had become too weak to walk very far. Her health had been failing for a long time. She was the victim of a little-known disease that attacked her nervous system. Milton and Kitty took trips to health resorts or to consult medical specialists, hoping that some doctor would have a cure. Unhappily, they did not find a cure, and in March of 1915, exactly two months short of their seventeenth wedding anniversary, Kitty died.

Milton was heartbroken. He resolved to devote his entire fortune to the school he and Kitty had begun together. It would be his monument to Kitty. As time went by, the Milton Hershey School, as it was later called, included girls as well as boys and graduated thousands of students.

(7)

What Chocolate Built

Although Milton devoted a lot of time, money, and energy to the school, he couldn't fill the emptiness he felt without Kitty. Milton hoped that travel would help make his grief a little lighter. His mother had always wanted to visit Cuba, so in 1916 he took her there.

Always thinking like a candy maker, Milton was interested in Cuba's largest industry—sugar. Milton decided to build a sugar mill there to guarantee plenty of sugar for the chocolate factory. He immediately put the plan into action, and soon the new mill was under construction. Just as he had done in Pennsylvania, Milton built a whole town for the workers. He called it Central Hershey, and he made sure there were homes as well as recreation for the people. He brought in doctors, dentists, and teachers. Milton built a railroad line to carry sugarcane to the mill and refined sugar to the port.

One day a tragic accident on the Central Cuban Railroad killed many people and left many children orphans. Again, Milton Hershey used Hershey, Pennsylvania, as a model and built a school for these children.

Though he spent his money on good things, Milton's mother was always a little afraid of his great wealth and always warned him of disaster. "Money can be made, but money can be lost as well," she told him. She insisted on working at her home wrapping candies every morning until her health began to fail. Milton devoted himself to her during her final months of life, and she died in 1920 at the age of eighty-four.

After her death, it seemed that Fanny Hershey's words would come true. Milton had real money troubles. The Hershey Chocolate Company was using so much sugar that the Cuban plant was not able to keep up, and Milton decided to buy sugar elsewhere for the future needs of the factory. He agreed to pay sky-high prices, assuming that the price of sugar could only go up and up. It didn't— it dropped dramatically.

When the sugar was finally delivered, Milton had to pay for it at the agreed-upon high price. He lost more than $2,500,000. Once again, Milton was forced to ask for a loan. The bank agreed, but only if they could send a manager to oversee things. Milton hated having someone from outside telling him how to run his business.

Milton vowed to pay the money back in record time. He asked his workers to put in extra-long hours to help pay off the loan, and they happily obliged him. Their boss had always been fair and generous with them, and now it was their turn to help him. Of course, Milton worked harder than anyone else. He trimmed expenses and found new markets for his products. He convinced the A&P stores, a chain of stores all across the United States, to stock his candy. This move guaranteed that HERSHEY'S chocolates would be sold all over the country at A&P stores. With everyone making an all-out effort, the bank loan was paid off in 1922. Milton triumphantly told the bank they could call off their watchdog, the manager.

For Milton Hershey, it had been a close call. He could have lost everything. He realized that the Hershey Chocolate Company was too big to be run by one man, so he split the company into three parts. One company would take care of the chocolate business, another would run the sugar operations in Cuba, and a third would run the town of Hershey, Pennsylvania. All three companies were controlled by the Hershey Trust Company, which supported the Milton Hershey School.

Throughout the 1920s, the entertainment attractions brought more and more visitors to Hershey. The chocolate factory prospered and began introducing new mouthwatering treats. In 1925 Hershey brought out MR. GOODBAR, a milk chocolate and peanut bar. Two new products hit the stores in the 1930s: KRACKEL, a chocolate bar filled with crisped rice, and HERSHEY'S MINIATURES, tiny versions of all the HERSHEY'S bars made.

Unfortunately, the 1930s brought more than new chocolate bars—they brought the Great Depression. The whole country was having financial problems. Many businesses went broke, factories began to lay off workers and to close, and even banks began closing. One-third of the workers in the United States lost their jobs.

The depression came to Hershey, Pennsylvania, too. Milton called a meeting of his top associates. He had a plan to make sure no workers would be laid off. He wanted to put people to work on building projects that would improve the city of Hershey. The company had enough money to pay for the new buildings, and with luck the depression would be over before too long. Milton's associates worried that the demand for chocolate might disappear, but Milton decided it was worth the risk.

Soon the town became a giant construction site. First the workers built the Community Building, complete with a theater, gym, swimming pool, and library. In rapid succession, they built a beautiful resort hotel, a sports arena, a stadium, a high school for the Milton Hershey School, and a modern air-conditioned office building for the company. All of this construction took care of the workers of Hershey. Although work hours were reduced, no jobs were lost.

Milton Hershey had gambled that the factory and town could survive the depression, and he was right. When the worst of the depression was over, the factory was back in full production again.

In 1937, when the world was gearing up for war, the United States Army came to Milton Hershey for help. The army wanted a chocolate bar for soldiers that would provide emergency food and wouldn't melt in a soldier's pack. The chocolate bar had to be small, yet able to keep a soldier going for a day.

This was just the kind of challenge Milton thrived on. He got his chief chemist, Samuel Hinkle, busy on the project. Soon Hinkle had perfected the FIELD RATION D chocolate bar. The "D" stood for "daily." Here was food for a fighting man for a day. The United States entered the Second World War in 1941, and before long, the Hershey Chocolate Factory was turning out half a million bars every day.

The United States government gave awards to factories and businesses that did something special for the war effort. Hershey Chocolate was awarded the Army-Navy "E" for excellence. Soon the flag with its proud "E" was flying over the Hershey factory.

Milton Hershey lived just long enough to see the United States and its allies win World War II.

60

Both Germany and Japan were defeated when, on October 13, 1945, Milton's long life of eighty-eight years ended. What a life of accomplishment it had been for a Pennsylvania farm boy. Today in the great rotunda of Founders Hall at Milton Hershey School stands a bronze statue of Milton Hershey with his arm around one of the orphan boys. Under the statue these words are written, "His deeds are his monument. His life is our inspiration."

Afterword

Milton Hershey had the right idea when he made Hershey, Pennsylvania, into a tourist town. People still love this chocolate town. In fact, four million people travel to Hershey each year. They can visit the amusement park and the zoo, and at the visitors' center they can learn exactly how cocoa beans become chocolate bars.

Milton Hershey would be pleased to know that more people than ever love his chocolate. The factory needs milk from about 50,000 cows—700,000 quarts—just for one day's chocolate production. Thirty-three million HERSHEY'S KISSES, along with many other chocolate products, are made each day. And ninety million pounds of cocoa beans are stored near the factory in twenty-four giant silos—enough to make 5.5 billion chocolate bars.

Milton would also be proud of the Milton Hershey School. About 1,200 students in kindergarten through twelfth grade now attend the school. Graduates have gone on to successful lives—some have even become executives of Hershey Foods Corporation. Milton Hershey once said, "If we had helped a hundred children it would have all been worthwhile." The Milton Hershey School has helped not just hundreds, but many thousands of young people.

Bibliography

Castner, Charles Schuyler. *One of a Kind.* Hershey, Pennsylvania: The Derry Literary Guild, 1983.

Malone, Mary. *Milton Hershey: Chocolate King.* Champaign, Illinois: Garrard Publishing Company, 1971.

Morton, Marcia, and Frederic Morton. *Chocolate: An Illustrated History.* New York: Crown Publishers, Inc., 1986.

The New York Times, November 9, 1923.

Shippen, Catherine B., and Paul A. W. Wallace. *Milton S. Hershey.* New York: Random House, 1959.

Snavely, J. R. *A Chat With Mr. Hershey.* Privately printed, 1932.

————. *Milton S. Hershey*—Builder. Privately printed, 1934.